Girl plus Pen

Doodle, Draw, Color, and Express Your Individual Style

by Stephanie Corfee

capstone

Craft It Yourself is published by
Capstone Young Readers
A Capstone Imprint
1710 Roe Crest Drive,
North Mankato, Minnesota 56003
www.mycapstone.com

Library of Congress Cataloging-in-Publication Data
Corfee, Stephanie, 1974- author.

  Girl plus pen : doodle, draw, color, and express your individual style / by Stephanie Corfee.

      pages cm. — (Craft it yourself)

  Audience: Ages 9-13.

  Audience: Grades 7 to 8.

  Summary: "Lively text and fun illustrations guide artists to create their own doodle artworks."— Provided by publisher.

  ISBN 978-1-62370-596-1 (pbk.) — ISBN 978-1-62370-597-8 (ebook pdf)

1. Pen drawing--Technique--Juvenile literature. 2. Drawing--Technique--Juvenile literature. 3. Doodles--Juvenile literature. I. Title.

  NC905.C67 2016

  741.2--dc23

                                        2015031705

Editor: Eliza Leahy
Designer: Lori Bye
Creative Director: Heather Kindseth
The illustrations in this book were created with ink, watercolors, and digitally.
Image credits: Stephanie Corfee

Table of contents

Anyone can doodle.

If you have something to draw with and something to draw on, you're in business. It's not about perfection. It's about uniqueness. For example, if you draw a wobbly circle, that is YOUR wobbly circle. There's not another like it! If you draw a lopsided horse with curlicue hair, it's one of a kind.

Drawing in ink encourages us to accept our imperfections and turn them into something beautiful.

I love that!

Sometimes I catch myself trying to perfect my doodles, and I immediately stop. You should too! Trust me, the first version is always the coolest anyway.

In this book, you'll find lots of step-by-step exercises. Those are not meant to turn you into a doodle robot! Those are to get you in the groove. As soon as you find your groove, go with it! And forget the steps! Move on and try some of the many ideas and inspiration pages designed to help you create your own doodles in your own way. I know you will draw amazing and original things. I've loved making this book, and I sure hope you will love using it!

XOXO
stephanie

Paint Pens
Opaque paint writes on practically anything with nice, vibrant color.

Doodle Tools

You don't need anything fancy to doodle. A plain old pen and paper work just fine. But here are some fun tools to try that are definite winners!

Gel Pens
These create fine lines in a rainbow of colors! Keep lots of white ones handy for adding doodles over darker colors.

Water Brushes
Water in the handle squeezes out to the brush! Perfect for adding watercolor effects to your permanent ink doodles – even on the go!

Mechanical Pencils
Always sharp, these draw like pens.
They're great for sketching outlines.

Pigment Ink Pens
A top pick for beautiful, detailed doodles
that are waterproof. You can find anything
from teeny point sizes to a juicy brush tip.

Ballpoint Pens
Just right for doodling
in your school notebooks.

Markers
These are super for coloring
doodles since the color won't
cover your doodled lines.

Loosening Up

Let your thoughts wander and draw whatever comes to mind. Your only goal here is to fill the page.

Doodling in color

Fill the spaces in the design on the opposite page using doodles from the palette below.

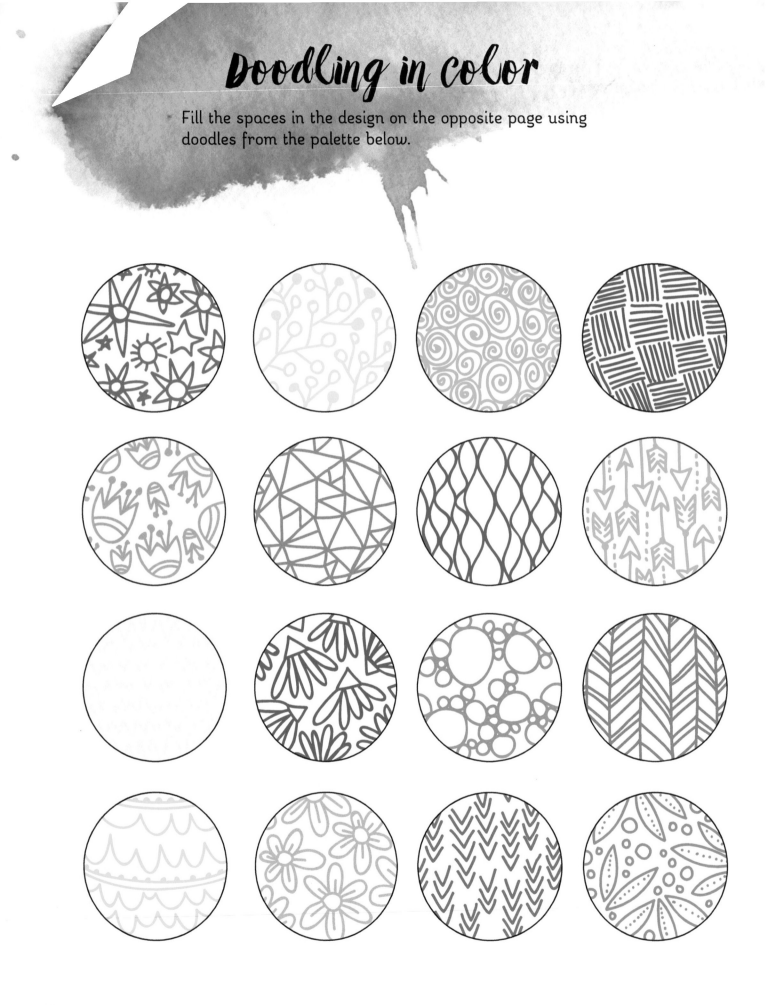

Doodle inside the colored bands using a white or
colored gel pen for texture.

Experiment with Borders

Make rectangular borders using the designs below, or create your own!

Creative Corners

Use the gray guides to help you create
your own fun doodle corners!

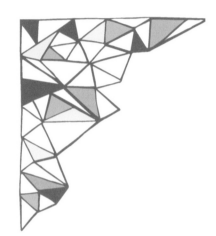

Twirls & Swooshes

Get your wrist nice and loose by scribbling circles and loops. Then practice the forms below, plus some of your own.

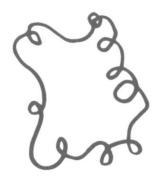

Lines, Shapes & Angles

Try your hand at geometric patterns like the examples below.

It's okay if your geometric doodles look a bit wobbly.
Resist the urge to use a ruler or straightedge.
Imperfections give it personality!

Doodle Clusters

A doodle cluster is a great way to decorate a label or the front of a journal. Start with a bold, large design in the center, then add medium-sized accents around it. Finally, fill in gaps with itty-bitty stars, dots, sparkles, or any doodads you like!

Frames & Wreaths

HAPPY

Tip:

Use a pencil to sketch the shape of your frame or wreath. Then doodle on and around it.

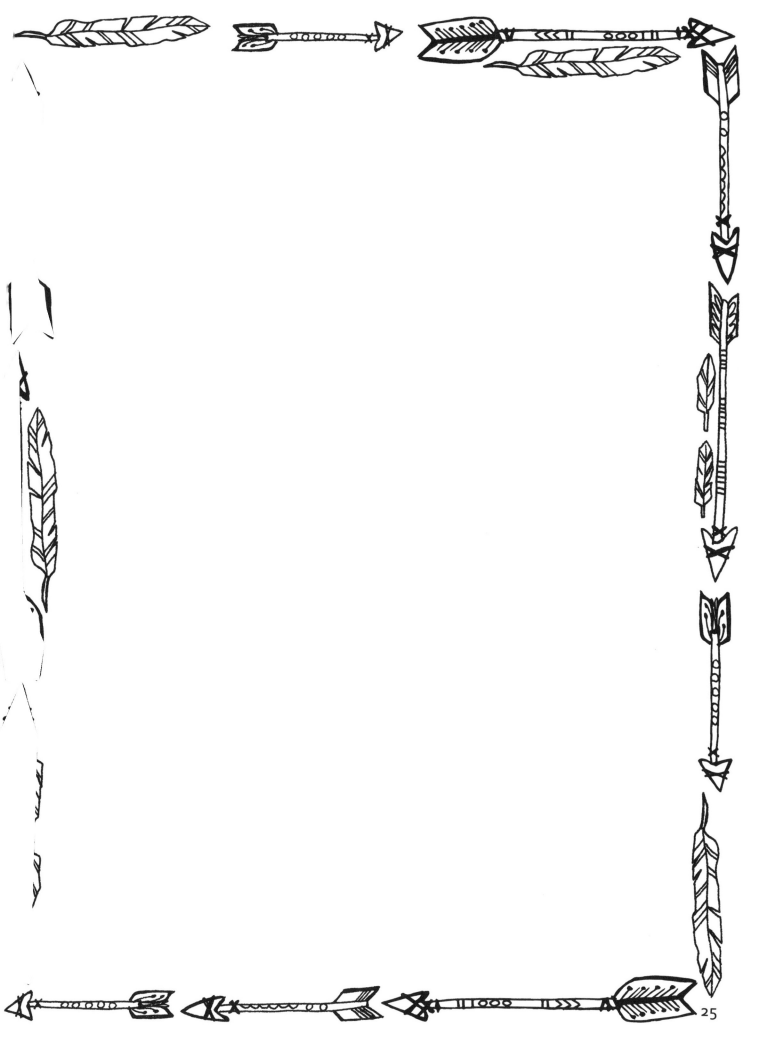

Doodle Your Name

Design your own on the facing page.

Doodle Free-for-All

Letters + Words

Letters and words top the charts as favorite things to doodle. We doodle our names. We doodle the names of our friends, pets, and even our secret crushes. It's easy! Add a few swirls, draw smiley faces over the *i*'s, and you've got some pretty cute and doodly words. But why not take it a step further? Try a doodle monogram with pretty, stylized letters. Make a fun poster for your room with a favorite catchphrase. Gain confidence in your lettering skills by tracing printed fonts from a computer. Once you've got the hang of it, start to transform your words into fun shapes. Then you can really decorate them with flair. Before you know it, all your friends will be asking for their names — doodled by YOU!

Doodle Your Favorite Nickname

Try doodling in watercolor for a fresh and feminine vibe.

Style your doodles to suit your nickname.

Doodle a custom Monogram

Doodle your favorite motto or catchphrase!

Alphabet doodles

Complete this doodle alphabet with your own unique letter styles.

Use this page to write words using your newly designed characters.

Decorative Nicknames

Use pencil guides to create perfectly aligned nickname artworks.

Use light pencil to sketch in curves if you'd like to add some shape to your lettering. Here, do two upward waves, then divide the space based on the number of letters in each word. It's a great guide!

Write the words in the template you've made. Thick letters give you the most area for doodling, so be sure to keep your lettering nice and chunky.

LOVE BUG

Doodle and decorate each letter!
Follow the example shown here,
or create your own designs.

ADD COLOR!
Try colors that suit the
person with this nickname.

Print Perfect
YOU ROCK

If you aren't confident in your lettering skills just yet, don't worry. Choose a font on a computer and print out your message at a good size. Then loosely trace the letters as you create your doodled artwork.

You don't need to trace the letters precisely, but you can use your printout as a guide to keep letters even and consistent in size. Feel free to add your own touches. Round the sharp corners, thicken the letters, add curves to straight lines — be creative!

Add as many doodles inside and outside the letters as you wish to make your message stand out!

ADD COLOR!

Markers work great over black ink doodles. They add bold color but don't cover the ink lines.

Dazzling Words

Add flourishes and decorations to simple lettering to make it pop!

Draw or trace a short word that describes you or a friend. Short words work best because we will be adding a lot of details and flourishes.

Add fun flourishes, tails, swooshes, and curls onto certain letters. You can even add a crown, a bird, or a heart to enhance the look.

Fill each letter and swoosh shape with fun doodles.

ADD COLOR!

Be sure to give each letter equally bold color so that none of them are left looking like they don't belong.

Try Your Own FUN Word Art

Doodles to Color!

Doodles are so excellent in black and white. But creating doodles to color is a pretty great idea. For one thing, coloring detailed designs is super-relaxing and a great way to unwind. You will get lost in the process, and before you know it, you'll have a masterpiece! Create lots of shapes and spaces in these doodles for color. Fill an entire page! If you use permanent black ink for these drawings, you'll be able to use any medium to color — markers, watercolor, gel pens, colored pencils, and more.

Complete this sugar skull doodle and then finish it with vibrant color!

Doodled Jewelry

Doodle your favorite designs
on each ring and bracelet!

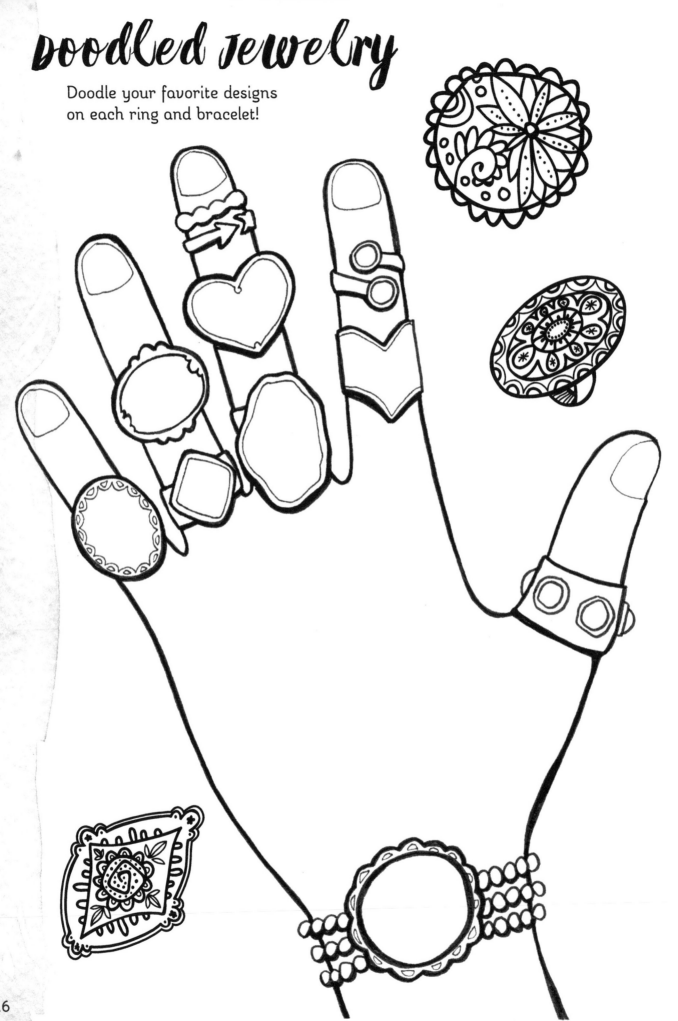

Butterfly Designs

Decorate your butterfly with any doodles you choose!

Lovely Leaves

Doodle designs on each leaf. Try not to repeat doodles. Challenge yourself!

Pretty Doodled Unicorn

Draw a whimsical unicorn with sparkles, flowers, hearts, and swirls.

Draw the basic shape of the unicorn's head. It's okay to trace the one here. It can be hard to draw horses!

Now it's time to add the horn — yay! Then add fun bits like a curly mane and cute decorations on the face and body. Be imaginative and think magical!

DOODLE IT UP!

Add fun doodles into every nook and cranny. Think about shapes that will look pretty on your unicorn, such as hearts, flowers, vines, sparkles, and scallops.

ADD COLOR!

I love to use watercolor and my favorite skinny water brush to color my doodles. But you can use colored pencils, markers, or even glitter paint!

Dream catcher

Make the circle form for your dream catcher and draw a dot in the center. Add bows on each side and some beaded strings on the bottom.

Add several curved lines from the center of the circle to the frame. Thicken the bows and add some feathers, beads, and doodles.

Add more curved lines from the center, but bending in the opposite direction. This is key! Complete with more doodles on the frame and feathers.

ADD COLOR!

Do you dream in color? Close your eyes and be inspired by the colors in your dreams . . . the many hues you might see in sunsets, rainbows, and fields of wildflowers.

Doodly Bicycle

Make lots of circles! Start with wheels, then make
a bike frame shaped like the letter M, and finally
add a bike seat and the handlebars.

Add the rest of the bike structures. Spokes on wheels are easy
when drawn like sunrays. Add pedals, baskets, and the first
outlines of your puppy and flowers.

Doodle the details! Finish the puppy and the flowers. Then decorate with dots, stripes, and swirls!

ADD COLOR!
Cheerful colors are a must for this bike! Or you can try choosing unexpected colors to add tons of personality!

Doodling Patterns

Building patterns with your doodles is so much fun. And you will amaze yourself with your creations. You can make coloring pages, greeting cards, or even wrapping paper that is one of a kind. The finished designs may look complex and impressive, but the process is amazingly simple. Patience is key. Create allover patterns by scattering large doodles across the page. Then add medium-sized companion doodles in the spaces between them. Finally, finish the pattern by filling the remaining gaps with simple dots, sparkles, or other tiny accents. Striped patterns are built up in a similar way, with lines placed first, and then filled with doodles from largest to smallest. Once you master the process, pattern-making will be your new favorite way to spend an afternoon.

Try doodling some detailed patterns.

Step-by-step

Create this sweet toss pattern by drawing the elements step-by-step, starting with the designs in pink! Follow with green doodles, and finally the purple. Add color if you like.

Tossed Patterns

Try some toss patterns of your own.

Sprinkle-Doodle Cone

Ice cream is even sweeter with pretty toppings like these!

Draw a skinny triangle with a band at the top. Add a backward s-type curve from right to left.

Add more rows of backward s curves. (Shown in yellow). Finish the swirl of ice cream as shown in red at the top and bottom. Add criss-cross lines on the cone.

Add the sprinkle-doodles! Doodle a different design in each section of the swirl. Finish with some tic-tac-toe marks and hearts on the cone.

ADD COLOR!
Go wild with colors beyond chocolate and vanilla! Make a rainbow swirl on a hot pink raspberry cone! This is your chance to get creative. What tasty ice cream can you invent with color?

Artsy Skateboard

Your style is one of a kind. Show it while you ride!

Make the outline of the skateboard and two circles for the wheels.

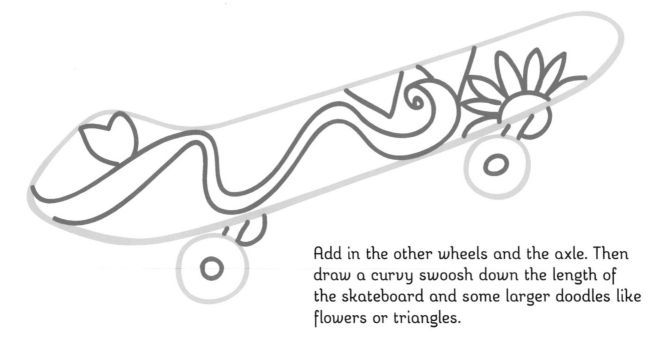

Add in the other wheels and the axle. Then draw a curvy swoosh down the length of the skateboard and some larger doodles like flowers or triangles.

Fill in all the spaces with smaller doodles and decorations and then add some twirly speed trails behind the wheels.

ADD COLOR!
Choose fun and energetic colors for your awesome doodled board that will make you want to ride!

Skirt Patterns

Fill each skirt with a fun doodle pattern. Think about using stripes, tossed patterns, or make up your own!

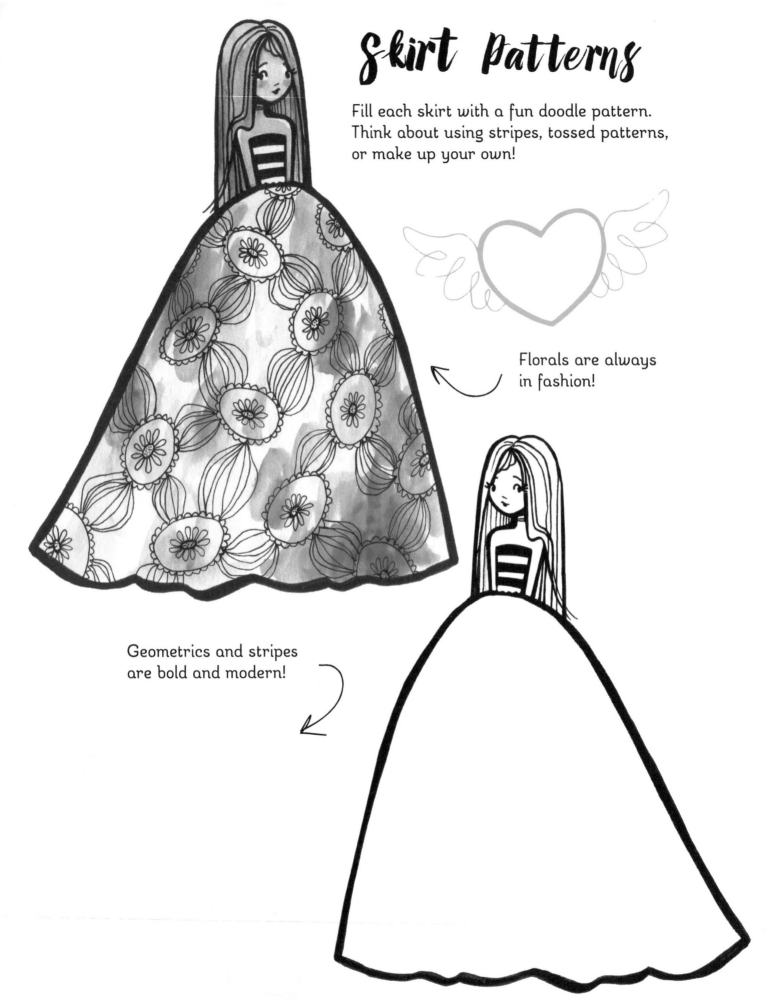

Florals are always in fashion!

Geometrics and stripes are bold and modern!

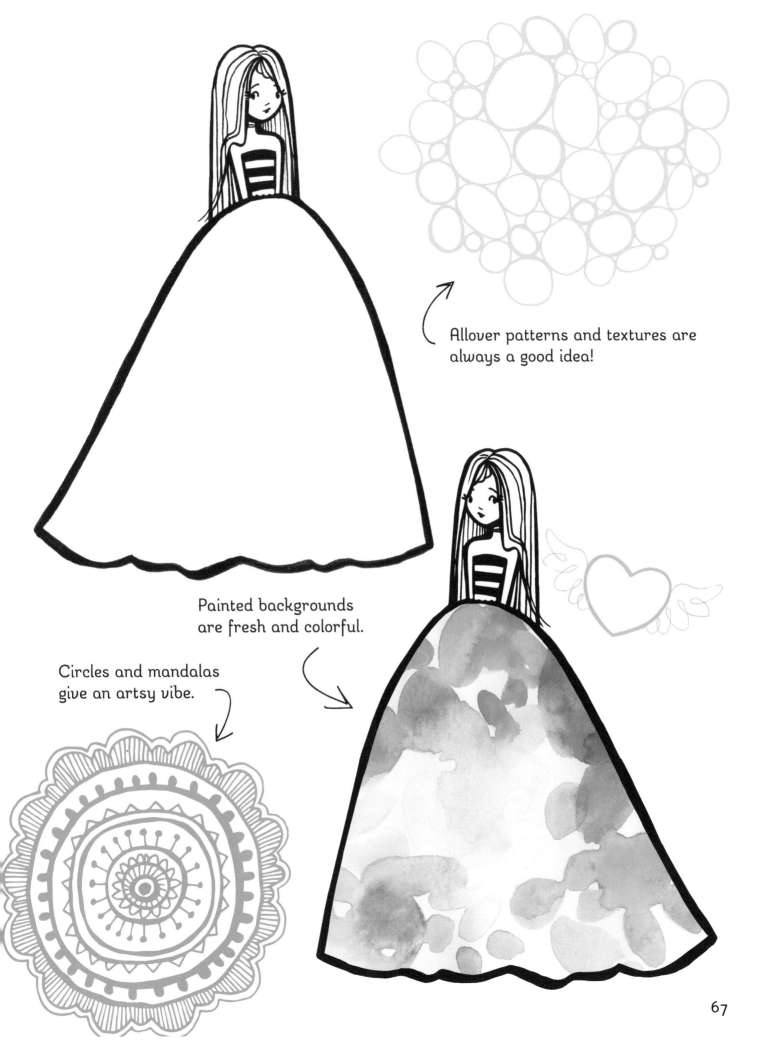

Allover patterns and textures are always a good idea!

Painted backgrounds are fresh and colorful.

Circles and mandalas give an artsy vibe.

Shape Up!

There are so many ways to doodle creatively. One of my favorite things to do is create familiar shapes using doodles. Simply draw the outline of a shape you love using light pencil, then doodle away with ink inside the lines! When you are all done, erase the pencil border and your doodle will look spectacular. Try a starfish shape filled with sea life doodles or an elephant shape full of floral doodles. These unique drawings make excellent gifts. If you know someone who likes to fish, you can make a fish-shaped doodle drawing for their birthday. For Valentine's Day, you can send cards with heart-shaped doodles. There are endless possibilities, so grab a pen and pencil and get to it!

Try Doodle-Filled Shapes!

Now try doodle-filled letters and words!

Make doodle-filled object silhouettes.

Fill each silhouette with a variety of doodles. Start with large doodles and then fill in the spaces with smaller and smaller ones. Try adding color!

Fill these extra feather outlines with doodles of your choice, like nature items or simple patterns.

Draw the outline of a favorite object — something that feels very YOU. Then fill the outline with doodles all about yourself. Add your name, symbols for your hobbies, a lucky number, or the name of your pet. Express yourself!

Doodle-design a tee and tote with your own special style.

Use this page to doodle accessories like hats, scarves, socks, and jewelry. It's your fantasy doodled wardrobe!

Are you a cat person? Use the above space to make some filled doodle shapes of the kitty cat variety!

Fill in the dachshund outlines with all kinds of fun doodles. Try sketching your pet's name or even draw a pup filled with flowers or sparkles!

Doodle an inspiring phrase of your own here. Think about tucking your lettering into a larger doodle shape, like the moon on the opposite page. The combination of lettering and images will make your work stronger than just one or the other.

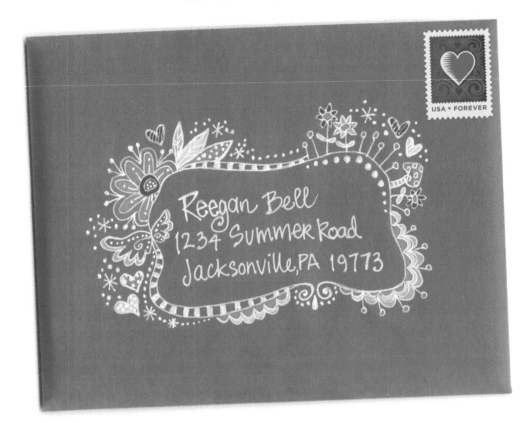

Reegan Bell
1234 Summer Road
Jacksonville, PA 19773

Can't Wait to Decorate

Doodlers often look at the world differently than other folks. They keep some pens handy and can't resist the urge to improve things. A plain old folder immediately gets transformed with a smattering of doodles. Book covers get ballpoint doodles and accents all around the title. Decorative doodling is a way to give all your random drawings some purpose. Add extra twirls and swirls to a birthday card envelope to make it special. Personalize a journal with unique borders. Add cute word bubbles to yearbook photos, then write in a memory. Sure, doodling is fun on a blank sheet of paper. But adding doodled decorations in unexpected places can help you take your creativity to a whole new level.

Decorate this menagerie with cute clothes, swirls, and doodads!

83

Doodle Designer

Decorate each charm to make a beautifully detailed bracelet.

Play with Your Food!

Decorate each part of this breakfast to turn them into fun characters!

Birdhouse Bliss

Design a doodle-decorated birdhouse for some feathered friends!

Customized Tunes

How would you decorate a ukulele to make it your own? Add flowers and swirls, your name, or even stripes and dots all over.

Music Makers

Doodle some other instruments and make them especially cute with doodle decorations. Try a harmonica, a trumpet, drums, or a pretty tambourine.

Shoe Lover

Design your own wedges below and then create a closet full of doodled shoes on the following page. Go beyond heels and create cool sneakers, flip-flops, and ballet flats.

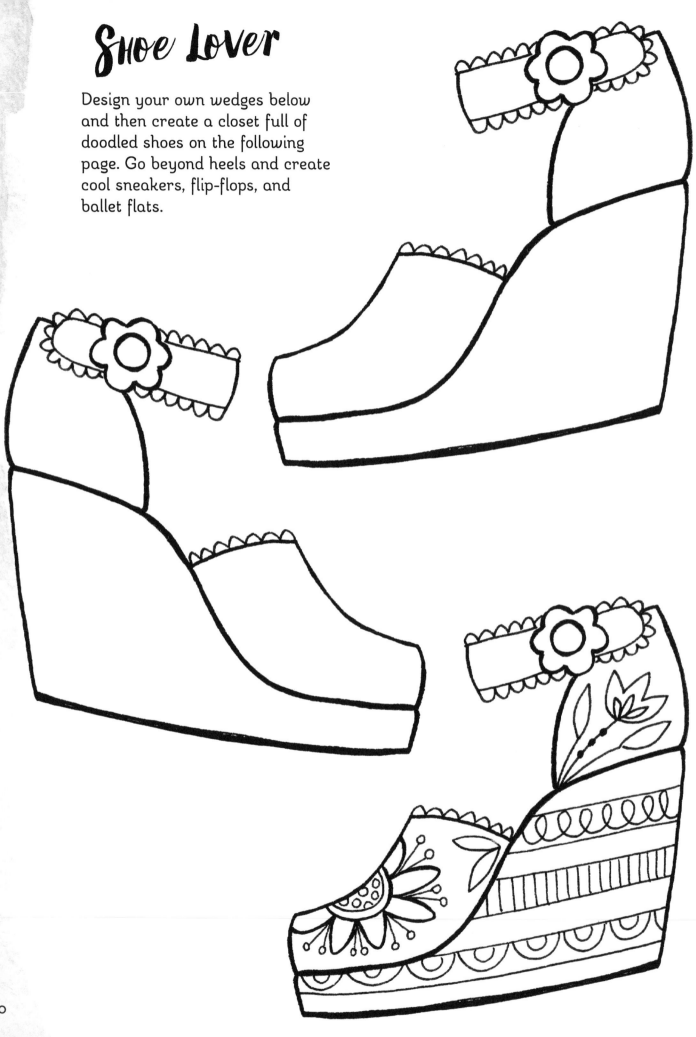

From Sky to Sea!

Fill in the page with beautiful birds, bugs, and butterflies.

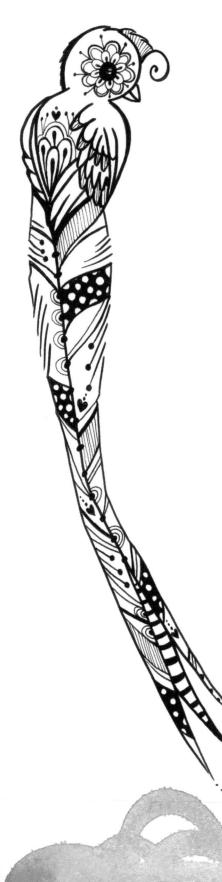

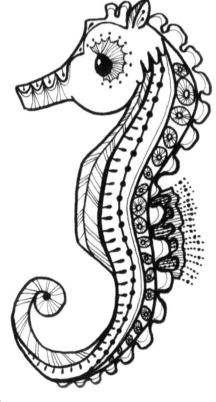

Use this page to try doodling sea life,
like jellyfish, starfish, an octopus, or a whale.

Daily Doodles

Keeping a sketchbook for daily doodles is an awesome practice. Drawing every single day takes the pressure off. When you become accustomed to making art so frequently, each drawing becomes more loose and spontaneous. That's when the "real you" — your unique artistic sensibility — emerges. Try to keep your journal or a small jot pad handy at all times. If you're caught without them, scribble on anything! Napkins, sticky notes, the backs of envelopes, or any old scrap of paper will do. Just tuck those into your journal later. You'll be surprised how quickly you fill a journal. You will also marvel at how much improvement you see from cover to cover. Don't try to be perfect, just get to doodling!

Circles with Style

Color in the doodle circles below, and then make some circle doodles with different themes. This one on the right will help you get started.

Signs and Banners

Doodle creative signs and banners with fun messages.

A Is for Artist

Choose a letter of the alphabet each day, then doodle as many different items as you can that begin with that letter.

Create an allover doodle on top of this vivid watercolor texture.

LOVE! LOVE! LOVE!

Doodle the word "love" three different ways. I've given you some inspiration below and a head start on the opposite page.

Try twisting vines and flowers around this script version.

Fill these faintly outlined letters with doodles.

Decorate inside these bubble letters with stripes, dots, sparkles, and more!

A Full Heart

Here is an intricate doodle-filled heart shape to color.
Create a large doodle-filled shape of your own on the
next page and finish it off with color too!

Now create Your Own Doodle Love!

Moonbeam Pendant

Doodle a magical pendant with your own wishing star.

Draw the main shapes of
the pendant and chain. Add
a crescent moon at the bottom.

Expand the main shapes with
fancy scallops, swirls, petals,
dots, and the wishing star.

Continue to expand each shape and curve by adding more scallops, rows of dots, and thin lines, plus some tiny antenna-like bits for fun.

ADD COLOR!

Tell a story with the colors you choose by thinking of a color inspiration before you begin. Use the colors of a favorite place, a bouquet of flowers, or a favorite dress. Your finished art will hold extraspecial meaning.

Create a cheerful umbrella with fun doodled panels.

Draw a simple umbrella shape and a puffy cloud as the base for your decorations and doodles.

Add a rainbow, cloud swirls, and raindrops. Then begin some doodles on the umbrella, including dots, scallops, and stripes.

Complete the doodled
umbrella panels.
Add a smiley face,
sparkles, and rainbow
stripes on the raindrops.

ADD COLOR!
A colorful umbrella
adds some brightness
to a gray day while you
wait for the rainbow.
Be inspired by rainbow
colors for this doodle!

I ♥ nature

Feathers + Leaves + Pebbles + Moonbeams = True Love

Draw your best, plumpest heart and add little slits and sticks where the arrow pokes through on each side.

Add doodles inside the heart — vines, the moon, pebbles, paisleys, and feathers. Also add the arrow tip and tail.

Add pretty details and doodles like hearts and sparkles. And add pretty touches on the arrow.

ADD COLOR!
Channel your inner earth goddess by choosing your spirit colors to decorate. Make it uniquely you!

Happy Doodles

What is a happy doodle? Happy doodles are the kind that you find yourself drawing again and again. They're your go-to doodles, the ones that flow effortlessly from your pen and give you a warm, fuzzy feeling. Maybe you always seem to draw pandas wearing bow ties. Maybe you lean toward florals or stylish fashion accessories. It's a lot of fun to look through your filled sketchbooks and try to note the themes that repeat themselves. Keep drawing those happy doodles! Happiness is the goal, after all. But on occasion, challenge yourself to doodle items OUTSIDE of your happy zone. If flowers are your thing, try drawing robots. If you love funky animals, switch it up to twirly lettering. Adding variety will make your awesome happy art even more interesting, engaging, and unique.

Dear Doodles

Doodle some favorite objects you have in your room!

Natural Expression

Doodle a few things you see as you walk outside.

Doodle some favorite gifts you have given (or received)!

No two people will draw the same group of things. In this exercise, celebrate your uniqueness! Doodle ten things that make you YOU. I've got you started with the first one.

10 things I love

I am a great Doodler

115

Flower Doodles

It's nearly impossible to talk about doodling motifs without mentioning flowers. Flowers are a tremendously popular subject. They are beautiful to draw and come in lots of interesting shapes and colors that beg to be inked onto the page. Twirling vines and leaves make perfect borders too! You can draw flowers from the garden, or you can get creative and draw flowers from your imagination. Doodled blooms filled with intricate decorations are fun to create and to color. Experiment with mixing large blooms and small ones. Try spiky leaves and looping vines. Draw a small circle and add rows and rows of petals to make an enormous blossom. You could fill a stack of sketchbooks with doodled flowers and still have plenty of ideas for more. How many can you imagine?

Fill this page with as many different flowers as you can.

Bring this garden to life with blossoms on each stem.

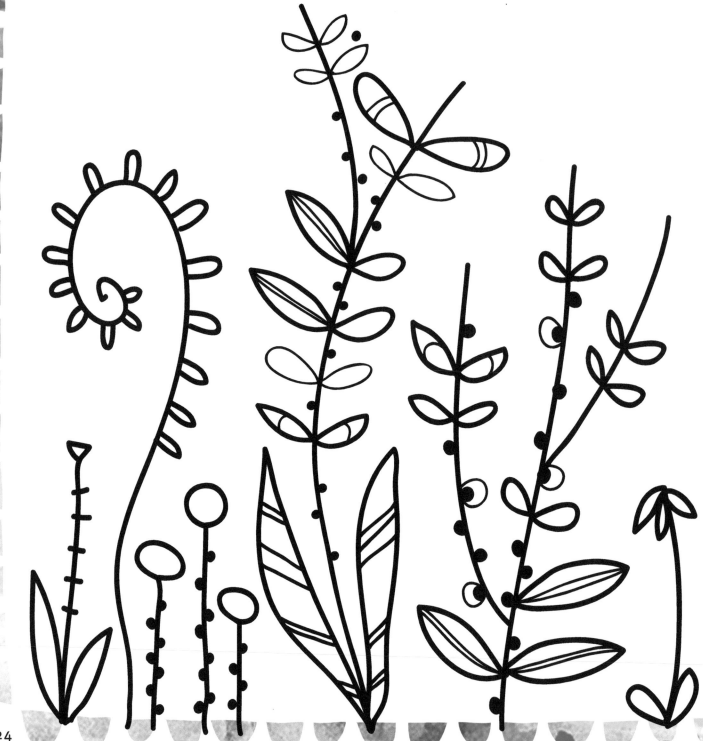

Complete the left side of the floral headdress and color it in!

Complete this crazy daisy with a different doodle design on each petal.

Lotus Love

Symmetry and pattern combine in this zen-tastic blossom.

Draw four leaves that resemble a butterfly. Make two large ones and tuck two smaller ones beneath.

Layer leaf-shaped petals above the butterfly. The pale pink ones go first, then add the dark pink. Last, add an outline all around and a tiny cluster of petals at center.

Doodle each petal and add long swirls for extradelicate detail.

ADD COLOR!

Harmonious colors are used on each petal. Harmonious colors are similar ones. For example, reds, pinks, and oranges are harmonious. These color combos glow with warmth and happiness.

Delicate little flowers jingle on a twirly stem with patterned leaves.

Draw a spiral stem. Add leaves and some flower stems all ready for their blooms.

Draw loopy, bell-shaped flowers on each stem and add some twirly tendrils.

Doodle fun and pretty details onto the pointy leaves, then add a few round leaves to finish things off.

ADD COLOR!
Blue is the undeniable color choice for the flowers here, but go crazy with the leaves and stems.

Funky Fleur

Unexpected, stylized petals and leaves add flair to this flower.

Draw an oval surrounded by round petals, and a stem with six leaves.

Make a tiny heart at the center, draw spirals on each petal and doodles on each leaf. Finish with leaves between the petals and a fun, knobby circle around the heart.

Add one last round of small details in the petals and leaves.

ADD COLOR!
Try dotting and speckling watercolor over your flower for a multicolor, textured look.

Try your own word art in the style shown on the previous page. Start with lettering at the center and then create a halo of doodles around it. Let some of the doodles fill in around the shape of the letters for a customized look.

Put It All Together

Use this spread to work on your favorite doodles!

Beyond the Pen

Doodling goes well with mixed media too!
Try doodling with a wide variety of fun and
easy-to-use tools all around you.

Nail Polish

Manicures are more fun with
a layer of doodles! Use a throwaway
thin paintbrush or ready-to-use nail
polish pens made just for decorating.

Fabric Markers

Decorate your clothing or
create unique stuffies with
your own style of doodles.
Simple fabric markers help
flirty flower skirts and detailed
animal stuffies come together
in a flash.

Icing Writers

Frosted cookies are the
perfect blank canvas for
sweet doodles made with
colored icing. It's doodle art
you can eat!

Needle & Thread

Embroider a simple pattern of doodles with a needle and embroidery floss. It's easy once you get the hang of it. Small hoops make a fantastic gift topper and larger ones are great on a door or wall.

Glitter!

Doodling in glitter will have you hooked. Just make your design with white glue, sprinkle with glitter, and let it dry. Can you say "sparkle"?

Craft Paint

A precious little canvas, a fine paintbrush, and patience are all you need to make these doodled masterpieces.

Wire

Find it in the jewelry section of the craft store. Can't you just imagine your name in wire? Make wall art, twirly earrings, or doodle drawings in 3D!

Puffy Paint

Add quick, textural designs to totes, sneakers, or backpacks with dimensional paint. Choose from tons of fun colors and finishes.

139

Off the page

Your doodles can make lots of things prettier! Just look around you and see all of the fun possibilities.

Doodle Scarf

Fabric or permanent markers can turn a plain scarf into something totally YOU. Wear it around your neck, in your hair, or knotted onto your bag!

Glasses Case

Any bare surface is fair game! Doodle your eyeglasses case so it's as cute as you!

Ring Dish

Doodle on little dishes or other pottery with a paint pen to make it your own.

Tip:

Terra-cotta pots and bowls from the craft store are inexpensive and come in many sizes. Just paint and doodle.

Canvas Hat

Doodle it your way! Permanent markers work perfectly. And your one-of-a-kind style will go with everything!

Wood Initial

A great touch for your bedroom door or wall. Markers are all you need!

Phone Case

Doodle on your case with permanent marker or upload your doodle to a print-on-demand website and place your order!

Doodled Pebbles

Add your touch to natural elements like river rocks, making for pretty decor or whimsical garden accents.

Photo Fabulous

Doodling your photos is so much fun. Grab some paint pens and get to work adding words, dates, and decorations!

School Memories

Doodle names and years on school pictures to make your memories supercute!

Add Some Style

Doodle colorful and over-the-top decorations, accessories, and accents that are sure to bring a smile.

Draw Some Detail

Add a touch of magic with drawn-on whimsical elements like wings, sparkles, and clouds to make sweet photos more like a fairy tale.

Share Your Emotions

Emojis aren't just for texting. These cute little guys tell it like it is.

Bon Voyage

Note the place and date in doodly style on your favorite vacation photos.

Fun Borders

Add rows of cute borders around any photo to give it an extra touch. Use colors to match the photo and make it pop!

Lovefest

Doodled hearts on photos are a classic. Bonus points for a heart-shaped photo cutout.

Add Some Silly!

Draw mustaches, glasses, funny eyebrows, rosy cheeks, and more to make your silly photos even sillier! These doodled snaps will make you laugh for years to come.

Best Friends forever

SISTERS = BEST XOXO FRIENDS

Go Be Creative!

No doubt your confidence and creativity have grown by
leaps and bounds by now. So break out some fresh, new sketchbooks
and get to filling them! Doodle every single day, and it will become a
very important part of you. And the books you fill will be
precious, one-of-a-kind treasures that nobody will
ever be able to re-create. Go you!